There Are Things I Don't Know

John Manos

Illustrated by Susan Aiello

Rigby®

Level R Guided Reading Chapter Book

On Our Way to English: *There Are Things I Don't Know*

© 2004 by Rigby
1000 Hart Road
Barrington, IL 60010
www.rigby.com

Text by John Manos
Illustrated by Susan Aiello

09 08 07 06 05 04 03
10 9 8 7 6 5 4 3 2

Printed in China

ISBN 0-7578-4527-4

I don't want to move.
I don't want to go.
I don't want to leave
Everything that I know.

They tell me I'll like it,
But I don't think so.
I don't want to move.
I don't want to go.

June 15

I think I'll run away.

I'm writing this diary to keep a record of my summer. I want to be able to reread my diary to remember the worst thing *Mamá* and *Papá* ever did to me: making me move!

We were enjoying a perfectly nice dinner tonight when they suddenly delivered the terrible news that we're going to drive down to my grandparents' farm in Texas in three days! *Mamá* and *Papá* will come back to Chicago to sell our house, but I have to stay with *Abuelo* and *Abuela*.

I was furious when they told me, and I even started shouting. I know I upset *Mamá* because she said, "We don't shout in this house, Manolo Campos." Usually she calls me Manny, and she never uses my whole name unless she's very angry.

June 17

I argued with *Mamá* and *Papá* again today, because it's not fair of them to make me move. *Mamá* reminded me that as *Abuela* and *Abuelo* get older, they need more help around the farm. I know she worries about her parents and misses them, but why can't they move here? I'm happy here in Chicago, so why should I have to go to south Texas just because *Mamá* and *Papá* want to? *Papá* told me that change can be good. *Papá* grew up in Chicago, and he'll miss it, too, yet he's happy about going to live where we have so many relatives. He'll be able to work as an electrician anywhere, and *Mamá* is going back to school to become a nurse. But I don't want to leave Chicago and my friends, and I don't want to go to a new school. I'm going to be miserable!

June 19

After three endless days of driving across the hot, flat countryside, we finally arrived at *Abuela* and *Abuelo's* farm this afternoon. When I got out of the car, *Abuela* hugged me tightly, and *Abuelo* shook my hand. Moving to a new place is difficult enough, but to make things even worse, *Abuelo* and I sometimes don't get along because he likes to tease me. For example, *Abuelo* refuses to call me Manny, and instead he calls me Manolito, like I'm a little kid.

The land here in Brooks County is just about as flat as Chicago, but it's very dry, and there are hardly any trees! The one good thing about the farm is Bronco, *Abuelo's* faithful, old dog. As soon as he saw me, he bounded across the field, threw his paws on my shoulders, and licked my chin happily with his tail waving in the air. *Abuelo* said that he hadn't seen Bronco move that quickly in years. I've always wanted a dog.

June 20

Today *Abuelo* showed me the fields where he grows cantaloupes and introduced me to the workers who help him. They've been harvesting the melons since May, and now they have to pull weeds and make sure bugs haven't hurt the melons. The melons stay fresh for only two to four weeks after being cut from the vine, so *Abuelo* sells them right away to the store that his friend Mr. Obando runs in town.

Abuelo showed me how to bend down, carefully pull up a melon, and see if it is ready to separate from the vine. If it pulls away from the vine easily, it is ready to be harvested. As hard as I tried, I couldn't keep up with the other workers, and I was straining under the weight of the melons, my back in terrible pain. *Abuelo* just laughed and said that working on a farm would make me stronger.

Feeling useless, I dragged myself to the barn where *Abuelo* was milking his cow, *Preciosa*, and told him that I was exhausted. *Abuelo* glanced at me over his shoulder, shook his head, and laughed, saying, "On a farm, Manolito, there is no time to be tired." Why does it seem like he's always laughing at me?

I don't like it here. It feels like the melon fields and the garden are the only interesting things to look at, and there aren't any places to go. I miss my friends in Chicago and walking to the store or going to a movie whenever I want. There's nothing for me to do on a farm.

June 25

Mamá and *Papá* drove back to Chicago yesterday, and I wished that I could have gone home with them. I didn't want to cry, though, so I just waved when they drove away.

Just then Bronco walked over and bumped my hand with his head, as if he knew how I felt. He is the only good thing about Texas.

June 26

Abuelo says that everyone has to work on a farm. I don't mind doing chores, but when I was carrying a bucket of milk from the barn to the house, I tripped on something—probably my own two feet—and spilled the entire bucket of fresh milk all over the path. *Abuelo* didn't yell at me, thankfully, but I could tell he was upset.

I said that I didn't understand why we couldn't just buy milk at the store. *Abuelo* stared at me for a minute and then said, "That isn't the way we do things on a farm." I wanted to tell him, "It's the way we do things in a city!" Although those words were running through my head, I knew better than to be disrespectful to *Abuelo*. *Mamá* and *Papá* would be so disappointed in me if I ever said something like that, so I didn't say anything at all.

Another one of my chores is to water the garden where *Abuela* grows beans, corn, and tomatoes. My job is to let the right amount of water flow into different parts of the garden. It's important that I pay attention to what I'm doing because water is limited here. It doesn't rain as much here as it does in Chicago.

June 27

After the awful week I've had here on the farm, I decided to call *Mamá* and *Papá* tonight. I feel so homesick, and even though I'm still not happy about their decision to move, I wanted to hear their comforting voices. I felt very lonely after I hung up the phone, but then *Abuela* and *Abuelo* said they wanted me to see something outside.

Abuelo said, "Just watch as the sun sets." Soon the colors of the ground and the thin, twisted trees all around us started to change. Under the bright daylight, the earth looks so dry, with pale grasses covering it like a carpet. But as the sun set, the air seemed to turn orange, the shadows grew blue and purple, and the sky glowed pink and red. It was beautiful!

June 29

Today was an amazing day!

Abuelo said I could take Bronco exploring with me, so we hiked through the plains to look at all the thorny plants and short, dry grasses that grow there. Just as we walked into an arroyo—a creek whose water has dried up from the heat—I came face to face with a javelina! As the small but fierce javelina lowered its head and curled its lip, a low growl rising from its throat, I knew it must have felt trapped.

Before I had time to decide what to do, Bronco ran past me and attacked the javelina! They rolled around and around on the ground until Bronco bit the javelina, and the javelina suddenly ran away. But Bronco had a deep cut on his back, and he couldn't even stand up.

I didn't know what to do, but I put my shirt on the cut and tied the sleeves tightly to make a bandage on Bronco's wound. Then I put Bronco up on my shoulders where he felt like a ton of bricks.

Abuela and *Abuelo* came running toward us when they saw me carrying Bronco. They thought I was hurt, but the blood they saw was Bronco's. *Abuelo* carried Bronco to the truck to take him to the vet, and *Abuela* led me inside to take a bath.

Exhausted from today's adventure, I forced myself to stay awake until *Abuelo* and Bronco returned. *Abuelo* carried Bronco into my room, and I saw that Bronco was wearing a bandage on his back. He looked much better, and *Abuelo* said that Bronco would be OK. *Abuelo* let Bronco sleep in my room, which is a special treat because Bronco isn't usually allowed to sleep in the house!

June 30

This morning *Abuelo* said Bronco weighs as much as I do. *Abuelo* was surprised I could carry Bronco out of the arroyo, across the plains, and all the way back to the farm. I told *Abuelo* I couldn't leave Bronco injured and alone. Then *Abuelo* looked at me for a long time and said, "I can see there are things I don't know about you." I didn't know what to say after that, but hearing it made me feel good.

Then he called me Manolo and invited me to play dominoes with him. "You're not going to call him Manolito anymore?" *Abuela* said.

Abuelo answered, "A man should be called by his grown-up name." Then he looked at me and smiled.

We spent most of the day sitting on the porch playing dominoes. *Abuelo* told me that when he was my age, he played dominoes with his *abuelo* all the time.

July 2

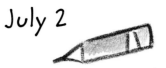

Texas is much hotter than Chicago, but the rain that fell today helped me feel cooler. *Abuelo* was worried, though, for if the melons get too wet, they may rot and spoil. It was raining too hard to do many chores, but *Abuelo* said that *Preciosa* still needed to be milked and fed. At home I'd probably just watch TV or read a book on a rainy day like today, but there's always work to do on a farm.

July 3

Abuelo said that even though the sun was shining today, we wouldn't be harvesting melons. The skin of the melons gets ruined if the melons are picked while they are wet. *Abuelo* said that once we finished our chores, we were going fishing!

Abuelo and I drove down the bumpy, dusty road to a nearby creek where the water sparkled in the brilliant sunshine and the trees swayed gently in the breeze. *Abuelo* showed me the best place to fish, and I caught three fish before we had our lunch! *Abuelo* told me that I might be a better fisherman than he is!

July 4

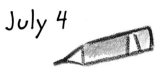

Today was wonderful because we went to an Independence Day barbecue at a farm about 20 miles away from ours! There were many people there, including four of my cousins—Blanca, Alonso, Vita, and Rumaldo—who are about my age. Everyone brought food, and I ate until I almost couldn't move.

Abuela made her famous tamales because I'm here. She said that it takes a lot of work to make her delicious meat filling and to wrap the tamales in corn husks, so she only makes them for special occasions. She worked on them all day yesterday to prepare for today's celebration. When she brought out the pans of tamales, everyone cheered! Vita said that *Abuela* makes the best tamales in Brooks County.

My cousins are all very nice, and they asked me to tell them about Chicago. Telling them about where I used to live made me feel less homesick.

July 10

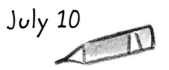

This morning *Mamá* told me our house in Chicago had been sold, and my whole world came to a stop. All this time, I had been hoping that our house wouldn't sell and we would have to stay in Chicago. I started to cry because now I can never go back home. When *Mamá* told me she missed me, I wanted to shout, "I don't care!" She said that she and *Papá* would drive down here soon to find a new house, and that made me cry harder. I'm not happy in Texas and I don't want to stay here! I almost said that to *Mamá*, but she already knew how I felt.

Usually *Abuela* and *Abuelo* don't like it when I get upset with *Mamá* or *Papá*, but this time they didn't say anything. *Abuelo* came out on the porch and stood there with me. After a few minutes, he said, "Well, let's go do our chores."

During dinner *Abuelo* asked if I would like to go with him on a few trips so that I could see more of Texas. That sounded OK to me.

July 11

Since it looks like I'm stuck here and there's not much to do, I decided to spend the day driving through Texas with *Abuelo*. We left the farm right after breakfast, and we didn't come back until it was time to milk *Preciosa* in the evening.

We loaded the back of *Abuelo's* truck with melons, and then we drove toward the Río Grande (which means large river). First we made a stop at Mr. Obando's store to deliver some melons, and Mr. Obando showed me how the people shopping in his store can tell if a melon is ripe. They sniff the melon to see if it smells sweet, then gently press on the stem. If the stem feels soft, the melon is ripe! Mr. Obando told me that these were the best melons *Abuelo* had brought him all summer.

Then we visited other farms and houses so that I could meet more friends and relatives. At every stop, we gave the people some melons and stayed to talk for a few minutes. All of *Abuelo's* friends wanted me to feel welcome and told me how happy they are that we're moving here. I'm not as happy about it as they are, but they were so nice to me.

When we got to the Río Grande, I remembered that the Chicago River flows through the middle of the busy city and has towering skyscrapers and streets overflowing with cars, buses, bikes, and people around it. But the part of the Río Grande we saw today is in the middle of the country and is surrounded by pale grasses and green bushes for as far as the eye can see.

On the way back, I told *Abuelo* that I wished Bronco were with us. *Abuelo* said Bronco is getting too old to ride around in the truck all day, but he would be waiting for us when we got home.

July 15

After we finished our chores this morning, *Abuelo* took me to the beach. On the way we stopped in a city called Falfurrias, where *Mamá* and *Papá* want to buy a house. The houses looked nice, and I even saw a few kids about my age playing outside. Then *Abuelo* showed me the school I'll attend if we move there, and it had a great baseball field in the back!

After that we drove to Kingsville so that I could see where *Mamá* will go to school. Then we drove to a beach where Bronco and I went swimming. It was so warm in the bright, Texas sun, and we found such a great place to swim. In Chicago, Lake Michigan is usually too cold for swimming, even at this time of year, so maybe there *will* be a few good things about living here.

July 20

Last night *Abuelo,* Bronco, Alonso, Rumaldo, and I spent the night outside! We put a sheet of plastic on the ground and slept in sleeping bags.

We watched the stars for a long time. In Chicago the night sky is bright from the glow of all the streetlights, but here the sky is clear and dark and covered with stars, and fireflies—not light bulbs—brighten the night! At home I got used to the noise of cars constantly speeding down the street, but here we listened to the sounds of the toads and insects.

After I turned off *Abuelo's* lantern, we told scary stories. Every time we heard a noise, Rumaldo or Alonso would get frightened. I would have been afraid, too, but I had Bronco lying next to me all night. Whenever I got scared, I reached out to pet him and felt his tail wag against my leg. *Abuelo* looked at me and smiled, and I knew we were safe.

July 23

Abuelo saved me from drowning today!

Because it was raining again this morning, *Abuelo* wanted to check the waterway that brings water to the melons. While we were next to the waterway, I leaned too far over, and suddenly I fell in! I tried to scream, but water flooded my mouth.

Then I felt *Abuelo's* big hand grab the back of my shirt, and I realized that he was in the water, too. He lifted me above the water and held me up while the current swept us along. Then he caught a tree branch that was hanging over the waterway, lifting me onto the ground and climbing out after me. We were soaked and muddy, our clothes heavy with the weight of the water, and *Abuelo* was breathing hard. Once I stopped choking, I looked at him and said, "I can see there are things I don't know about you." That made him laugh, and he hugged me tightly.

July 24

Patricio, my best friend from Chicago, is coming to see me! *Mamá* and *Papá* are bringing him when they drive down here next week to look for a new house, and I can't wait to show him everything!

July 30

Patricio, *Mamá*, and *Papá* arrived tonight, and although I was glad to see *Mamá* and *Papá*, for some reason I refused to tell them. I guess I'm still a little upset with them for making us move.

August 6

Patricio's visit wasn't like I'd hoped it would be. He laughed at the people here, just because he's from the city and they aren't. I couldn't believe that Patricio thought he was superior to the wonderful people around here.

He complained that they don't have many different restaurants here and that they can't catch a bus to see a movie or go to a major league baseball game. I like those things, too, but now my list of great things to do is longer than Patricio's because I've also lived in the country.

I told Patricio that there might not be as many movies to see around here as in Chicago, but that I've seen the stars covering the sky like a blanket of fireflies. And the country may not have as many restaurants as Chicago, but I'd much rather eat *Abuela's* warm, meaty tamales than a fast-food burger. And I don't miss the rumbling sound of buses driving down the street around Chicago. I like being able to hear the chirping of insects and the blowing of the wind here. Sure, I still miss the city, but if I left Texas now I'd miss the country and all of my new friends.

Patricio listened to everything I said, but he didn't seem to believe me. Now I'm sad, for I feel like I've lost a friend. And, unfortunately, I was glad when Patricio left.

August 25

Mamá and *Papá* will arrive tomorrow to stay, and they found a nice house in Falfurrias that is only two blocks away from my new school. After all this time, now I don't want to leave the farm, so I asked *Abuelo* if Bronco could come with me. *Abuelo* replied, "I know you love that dog, and he loves you, too. But Bronco is too old to make a move like that. You can come to visit him anytime you'd like, but he would have a hard time getting used to living in a new place."

Abuelo added, "Moving to a new place is difficult, isn't it?" I nodded because now I know how difficult it is.

I went over to where Bronco was lying on the porch, and I hugged him with my face pressed into his neck. He wagged his tail at me like he always does, and that made me sad all over again.

August 28

When I got up this morning, *Abuela* looked at the calendar and reminded me that summer vacation is almost over. She asked me if I would miss going back to school with my friends in Chicago. I couldn't answer her then, but I've been thinking about my answer all day.

Living in Chicago was like living in a carnival with colored lights and nonstop sound, constant motion, and the endless activities of millions of people. It never stops, and there is always something to do.

Living in the country, though, gives me time to really look around and to pay attention. There are things in the sky—different types of clouds and streaks of sunset color—that I've never seen before. I'm sure that in Chicago there are many small, interesting things happening, just like here, but I didn't see them before.

Two months ago I felt sad and angry. But my time here has changed a lot of things since I left Chicago in June, and I have changed more than anything else. I think school here will be a new adventure, and I'll tell *Abuela* that in the morning.